WORDS FROM THAT PLACE AT THE EDGE OF MEMORIES AND DREAMS

Copyright © 2025 by Carl Hansen

All rights reserved.

ISBN 978-1-62806-456-8   (print | paperback)

Published by Salt Water Media
29 Broad Street, Suite 104
Berlin, MD 21811
www.saltwatermedia.com

Cover image used with permission/license from istockphoto.com

WORDS FROM THAT PLACE AT THE EDGE OF MEMORIES AND DREAMS

C. H. HANSEN

CONTENTS

Just Be 8

Morning Glory 10

Equinoxes 11

Only Our Eyes Can Speak of That 12

The Enigma of Paradox 13

The House on Carol Avenue 14

Forever Ended Yesterday 15

Prayer 17

Psalm 18

A Life and A Day 19

A Door Only I Could See to a Room that Had Yet to Be 20

JUST BE

In my life love had died.
No. Rather it had been so badly
wounded it could not survive .
I could not unsee.
I could not unhear.
   I could not unremember.
   I could not unbe.
   I could not unfeel.
The wound was too deep ever to heal.
The sorrow too heavy a burden to bear.
I lost my faith in love.
I lost my desire to care.

For the first time in years, I
went down to the ocean,
not knowing what I expected to find.
Perhaps I just wanted to reboot my mind.
A young woman, passing on the street,
whom I had never met and would never meet,
saw my expression and admonished me,
"Smile. It's summer. It's the beach
Feel the sun and smell the sea.
Let it all go and just be.

Her random act of kindness,
Her unexpected remark,
Broke through my self-pity
And touched my heart.

But before I could think of what to say,
She smiled at me and went on her way.
And then I saw you on that very same day.
You stepped on to the boardwalk from out of my past,
And I knew the hurt was ending at last.

When I hear the cries of the gulls and
 the sound of the surf on the sand,
I remember the young woman on the street,
whom I had never met and would never meet.
And I remember her smiling at me.
I remember you on the boardwalk and the
warmth of the sun and the scent of the sea,
and I remember those words that seemed so
touching to me,
"Feel the sun and smell the sea. Let it all
go and just be."

MORNING GLORY

You are the Morning Glory who brings joy into my days,
because you have been here for me in oh so many ways.

You saw a wounded heart and mended it.
You saw my hurt and ended it.
You saw my life in pieces and reassembled it.

You are the Morning Glory who puts splendor in my days,
because you are so beautiful in oh so many ways.

I saw your caring heart and mine began to mend.
I saw your joie de vie and my hurt had to end.
I felt your love surround me and I had a life again.
You are the Morning Glory; you bring splendor to my days.
You are so much more beautiful than all my words can say.
You are the Morning Glory; you bring splendor to my days.
You are so much more beautiful
then all my words can say.

You are the Morning Glory; this song's my gift to you.
It can't come close to you in beauty, but
it's the best that I can do.

EQUINOXES

   At the end of the last Summer day,
we watched the sun set across Isle of Wight Bay.
The fading blue sky was cloudless and clear,
the western horizon a red lipstick smear.
The bay was calm; not a wave, not a ripple, not a whisper,
not a splash;
and without any warning came an emerald green flash.
Then the sun vanished, leaving twilight behind,
and us standing together, your hand in mine
We faded away with the last of the light.
And then we were gone with the coming of night.

   At the dawn of the first Spring day,
We stand on the beach and watch the night fade away.
To the east, the sky begins to brighten.
Above, the stars start to fade as the sky begins to lighten.
The ocean is calm, the sound of the surf just the
gentlest splash,
when suddenly from the east shoots an emerald green flash.
Then the sun breaks the horizon line
dragging a golden dawn up behind,
as we stand on the beach, your hand in mine.

ONLY OUR EYES CAN SPEAK OF THAT

I've been trying for the longest time,
to understand in my own mind,
just exactly how
we've come to know what we know now.

Deep in our brains where our souls abide,
deep in our hearts where love resides,
we know other lives future and past,
but only our eyes can speak of that.

Only our eyes are allowed to confide
the connection we feel deep inside,
and that our connection certainly transcends
the illusion that our lives have beginnings and ends.

Only our eyes can share what we know.
Since time out of mind it's always been so.
Forever is only a beat of our hearts;
the time granted us before we must part.

Only our eyes are allowed to convey,
The words we are forbidden to say.
Forever is only a beat of our hearts
Before we must part,
         Once more.

THE ENIGMA OF PARADOX

　　How is it:
That sometimes a whisper is louder than a roar?
That sometimes a single tear is more torrential than any storm.
That sometimes one word is more powerful than the most eloquent oration.
That sometime a smile is the most effective medication.
While on the other hand,
a laugh can do more harm than any poison can.
And sometimes love does more damage than all the hate that ever was.
That sometimes a paradox conveys a truth more clearly than the most perfect syllogism does.
That makes me ask myself, "What if",
a seeming contradiction is merely pointing the way to a paradigm shift,
　　to what will be rather than what was.
　　to a phrase that has yet to be turned.
　　to a lesson that has yet to be learned.
　　to a question that has yet to be asked.
　　to a truth that was previously masked by the misconceptions of the past.

THE HOUSE ON CAROL AVENUE

   Sometimes I see the house on Carol Avenue in
my dreams;
a neat, white Cape Cod surrounded by lawn and,
in front, a slender, young maple tree,
just as it was in 1953.

   I was seven,
and to me, growing up, that house on that street was heaven.
It was perfect in every way;
the place I grew up and expected to stay.
But when I grew up, life called away.

   The street and the house are still there,
another family's dream to share.
I don't go back now, but not because I don't care.
Rather it's because I want to believe they remain
the same,
and one day I'll hear again my mother call my name.

   Then it will be
late afternoon of a summer day in 1953.
And my parents will be
in the front yard waiting for me,
Just like they did when I was seven,
and then I'll know I've made it to heaven.

FOREVER ENDED YESTERDAY

   Wasn't it just yesterday
I was yelling for you to come out and play?
No, that was sixty years ago.
Yesterday you passed away.

   It seems like only yesterday
we walked to school together, you and I.
No, that was fifty years ago.
Yesterday was the day you died.

   It sure seems like only yesterday
we rode our bikes up Roger Street.
Into town. All the way.
No. I keep forgetting, you passed away
yesterday.

   Remember when we were fighting over that girl?
What was her name?
We were both fools. What can I say?
She dumped us both, any way.
Seems like yesterday.
But no; yesterday you passed away.

   I was your best man; you were mine.
We swore best friends forever; we toasted to that
many times.
But forever ended yesterday,
the day you passed away.

I woke up excited today
to go call for you to come out and play.
For a moment I'd forgotten that forever ended
yesterday;
the day you passed away.

PRAYER

   When I close my eyes to sleep,
the Universe the Lord will keep.
So in the morning when I wake,
the birds will sing and day will break;
another day of celebration,
thanking God for all creation.
So when night comes, I can sleep,
my heart at rest, my soul at peace.

PSALM

   You are the Lord of all that ever was, is,
Will be;
all planets and stars, and on Earth, all
lands and seas.
As in the beginning, You are the ONE.
God the Father, God the Spirit, God the Son.
Hallowed be thy name, Elohim, Yahweh, Jehovah, God;
all the same.
God the Father, God the Spirit, God the Son,
Holy Trinity, God the ONE.

A LIFE AND A DAY

   I expect to live a life and a day.
I know you'll be with men every step of the way,
so when I know not what to decide, I need
only look to You at my side.

It is easy to see in the clear light of day,
but much harder to see the way,
when the clouds gather and block the sunlight,
and when the storm breaks, turning day into night.

   Lightning flashes, rending black skies;
every flash blinding my eyes.
Thunder cracks, so sharp my ears are split,
as if by the kiss of an unholy whip.

   Wind-driven rain lashes my face,
I should be afraid but that's not the case.
I have nothing to fear.
I feel your presence; I know You're here.
   Then You tame the terrifying tempest,
and banish the frightful darkness to reveal a
perfect azure sky,
the wind's wild roar reduced to a sigh.

   I expect to live a life and a day.
The life will be as long as You say.
But the day, ah the day will be,
as promised by You, eternity.

A DOOR ONLY I COULD SEE TO A ROOM THAT HAD YET TO BE

   In my mind, in memories or dreams, it seems
for a thousand years,
plus a thousand years,
plus a thousand years,
and more,
I had been searching for
a long ago door
in a place I had been long, long before.

   In my mind, in memories or dreams, it seems
that I had sailed through the Pillars of Hercules,
passed Phoenician sands,
then eastward beyond Etruscan lands,
and along the Trojan shore,
through the Hellespont into the Golden Horn.

   In my mind, in memories or dreams, it seems
that I had gone ashore at Byzantium.
Then, joining a caravan,
I had traveled overland,
Far from the Golden Horn, to Angora,
Where I'd been long, long before,
Seeking that long-ago door,

   In my mind, in memories or dreams, it seems,
I found a door that wasn't there,
a midnight mirage,
a shimmering, moonlit fantasy,

that only I could see,
to a room that had yet to be,
and you waiting for me,
as if it was I whom you expected to see.

   In my mind, in memories or dreams, it seems,
We played and danced on Angora's streets,
Singing ancient songs
And waving at caravans coming and going.
We spoke about everything; of wars and peace,
love and hate, of gods both old and new,
of prophets and poets, even chores we hate to do.
And what it takes to make perfect stew.

   For a thousand years,
plus a thousand years,
plus a thousand years,
and fifty more,
we were oblivious to the passing time,
of being left behind,
outside the room that had yet to be,
to which there is no key.

   In my mind, in memories or dreams, it seems
I had lost the long-ago door
that I had been searching for,
a door only I could see,
a door that had no key,
to the room that had yet to be,
and in so doing, I lost you and you lost me.

And all that remains are memories and dreams.

ABOUT THE AUTHOR

C. H. Hansen was born in Baltimore. He is a graduate of Towson University. He resides in Ocean City, Maryland.

www.ingramcontent.com/pod-product-compliance
Lightning Source LLC
Chambersburg PA
CBHW041535070426
42452CB00046B/2968